COMPSOGNATHUS

BY SUSAN H. GRAY · ILLUSTRATED BY ROBERT SQUIER

The Child's World®

Published by The Child's World®
1980 Lookout Drive • Mankato, MN 56003-1705
800-599-READ • www.childsworld.com

ACKNOWLEDGMENTS

The Child's World®: Mary Berendes, Publishing Director
The Design Lab: Kathleen Petelinsek, Art Direction and Design;
Victoria Stanley and Anna Petelinsek, Page Production
Editorial Directions: E. Russell Primm, Editor; Lucia Raatma, Copy Editor;
Dina Rubin, Proofreader; Tim Griffin, Indexer

PHOTO CREDITS

©AVTG/iStock: cover, 2–3; ©Joseph Nettis/Photo Researchers, Inc.: 10–11;
©Biophoto Associates/Photo Researchers, Inc.: 12–13; ©Craig Lovell/Corbis:
15; ©The Natural History Museum, London: 18–19; ©Layne Kennedy/
Corbis: 19 (top)

LIBRARY OF CONGRESS CATALOGING-IN-PUBLICATION DATA
Gray, Susan Heinrichs.
  Compsognathus / by Susan H. Gray; illustrated by Robert Squier.
    p. cm.
  Includes bibliographical references and index.
  ISBN 978-1-60253-237-3 (lib. bound: alk. paper)
  1. Compsognathus—Juvenile literature. I. Squier, Robert, ill. II. Title.
  QE862.S3G6935 2009
  567.912—dc22   2009001623

Printed in the United States of America
Mankato, Minnesota
May, 2010
PA02063

TABLE OF CONTENTS

What was *Compsognathus*? 4

What did *Compsognathus* look like?. 7

What does its name mean?. 11

How did *Compsognathus* spend its day?. 12

How do we know about *Compsognathus*? 16

Where have *Compsognathus* bones been found?. . . 20

Who finds the bones?. 21

Glossary 22

Books and Web Sites. 23

About the Author and Illustrator. 24

Index 24

WHAT WAS COMPSOGNATHUS?

Compsognathus (komp-sug-NATH-uss) was one of the smallest dinosaurs. It only weighed about 7 pounds (3 kilograms). That's not much bigger than a chicken!

Even though Compsognathus was small, it was dangerous. Compsognathus was a good hunter with sharp teeth and claws.

6

WHAT DID COMPSOGNATHUS LOOK LIKE?

Compsognathus was a slim, little dinosaur. It had a thin neck and a long, **slender** tail. *Compsognathus* trotted around on two legs. It held its little arms up as it ran.

Compsognathus' *long tail helped it stay balanced as it ran. It was a very quick dinosaur.*

Although this dinosaur was small, it was a good hunter. It had tiny, sharp teeth. It had claws on its fingers and toes. *Compsognathus* ran around, chasing insects and lizards. It grabbed them with its mouth or its tiny hands. It munched them up with its itty-bitty teeth.

There were plenty of small creatures for Compsognathus to munch on. It did not hunt other dinosaurs, though. It was too small!

Sismasal

Lateral Temporal
Fenestra

Condyle

Dentary

WHAT DOES ITS NAME MEAN?

Compsognathus means "pretty jaw." **Scientists** gave the dinosaur this name because of its **delicate** bones. They were small and light. Its back and tail bones were very **fragile**. Arm and leg bones could easily be broken. **Skull** and jaw bones were also delicate.

Scientists use brushes and other tools to carefully loosen the rock around the bones.

HOW DID COMPSOGNATHUS SPEND ITS DAY?

Compsognathus hunted, ate, slept, and hid from other dinosaurs. Its sharp eyes spotted **lizards** as they darted about. Its little hands grabbed insects as they skittered by. This dinosaur probably did not eat very much. Something the size of a chicken did not need big meals!

Preserved plants such as these help scientists learn about what the weather may have been like when dinosaurs lived.

13

After eating, *Compsognathus* probably took a nap. It found a safe place where other dinosaurs could not find it. Being little came in handy. It was easy to find a good hiding place.

Scientists search for dinosaur bones in many places, including these rocks in France (above). Compsognathus' small size made it easy to find a safe hiding place (left).

HOW DO WE KNOW ABOUT COMPSOGNATHUS?

Compsognathus lived and died millions of years ago. Sometimes, other dinosaurs ate it. Sometimes, *Compsognathus* got sick and died. Then its small body just rotted away.

Compsognathus *had to watch out for bigger dinosaurs. If it wasn't careful, it would get eaten!*

18

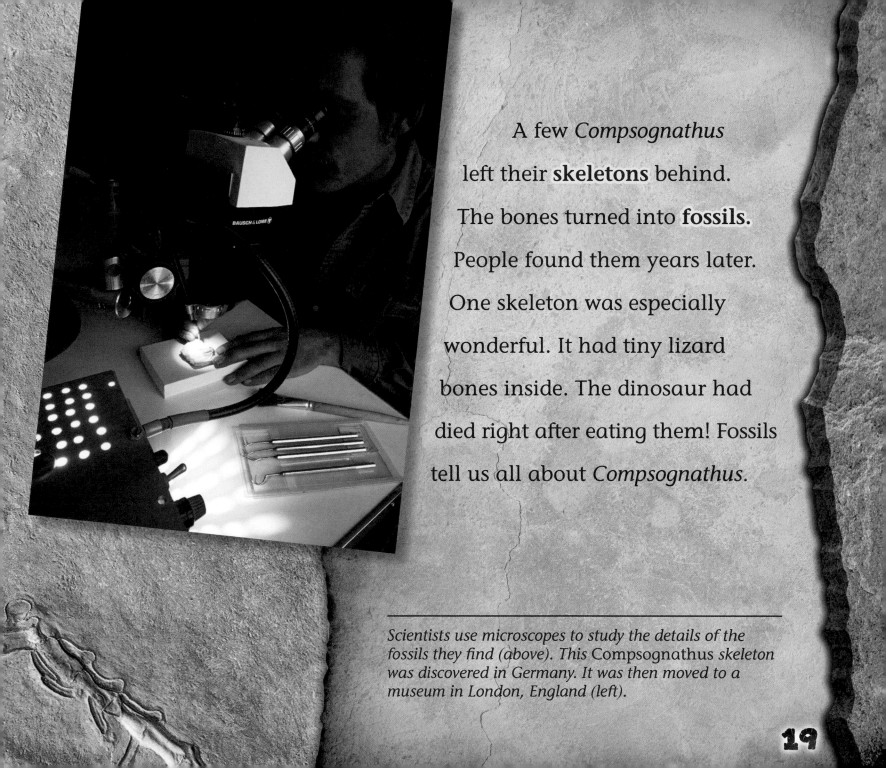

A few *Compsognathus* left their **skeletons** behind. The bones turned into **fossils**. People found them years later. One skeleton was especially wonderful. It had tiny lizard bones inside. The dinosaur had died right after eating them! Fossils tell us all about *Compsognathus*.

Scientists use microscopes to study the details of the fossils they find (above). This Compsognathus *skeleton was discovered in Germany. It was then moved to a museum in London, England (left).*

WHERE HAVE COMPSOGNATHUS BONES BEEN FOUND?

France

Germany

EUROPE

ASIA

NORTH
AMERICA

Atlantic
Ocean

Pacific
Ocean

AFRICA

SOUTH
AMERICA

Indian
Ocean

AUSTRALIA

Map Key

Where *Compsognathus*
bones have been found

Southern Ocean

WHO FINDS THE BONES?

Fossil hunters find dinosaur bones. Some fossil hunters are scientists. Others are people who hunt fossils for fun. They go to areas where dinosaurs once lived. They find bones in rocky places, in mountainsides, and in deserts.

When fossil hunters discover dinosaur bones, they get busy. They use picks to chip rocks away from the fossils. They use small brushes to sweep off any dirt. They take pictures of the fossils. They also write notes about where the fossils were found. They want to remember everything!

Fossil hunters use many tools to dig up fossils. It is very important to use the right tools so the fossils do not get damaged.

GLOSSARY

Compsognathus (*komp-sug-NATH-uss*) *Compsognathus* was one of the smallest dinosaurs that ever lived.

delicate (*DEL-uh-kut*) Delicate things are those that can be easily broken.

fossils (*FOSS-ullz*) Fossils are preserved parts of plants and animals that died long ago.

fragile (*FRAJ-il*) Fragile things can be damaged very easily.

lizards (*LIZ-urds*) Lizards are scaly animals that walk on four legs.

scientists (*SY-un-tists*) Scientists are people who study how things work through observations and experiments.

skeletons (*SKEL-uh-tunz*) Skeletons are the sets of bones inside bodies.

skull (*SKUHL*) The skull is the set of bones in the head.

slender (*SLEN-dur*) Slender things are things that are thin.

BOOKS

DK Publishing. *First Dinosaur Encyclopedia.*
New York: DK Children, 2006.

Gray, Susan. *Compsognathus.*
Mankato, MN: Child's World, 2005.

My Terrific Dinosaur Book.
New York: DK Publishing, 2008.

Parker, Steve. *Dinosaurus: The Complete Guide to Dinosaurs.*
New York: Firefly Books, 2003.

WEB SITES

Visit our Web site for lots of links about *Compsognathus*:

CHILDSWORLD.COM/LINKS

*Note to Parents, Teachers, and Librarians: We routinely verify our Web links to make
sure they are safe, active sites—so encourage your readers to check them out!*

INDEX

arms, 7, 11

bones, 11, 19, 20, 21

claws, 8

eyes, 12

fingers, 8
food, 8, 12, 19
fossils, 19, 21

hiding, 12, 15
hunting, 8, 12

insects, 8, 12

jaws, 11

legs, 7, 11
lizards, 8, 12, 19

map, 20

neck, 7

size, 4, 12, 15
skull, 11

tail, 7, 11
teeth, 8
toes, 8
tools, 21

weight, 4

ABOUT THE AUTHOR

Susan Gray has written more than ninety books for children. She especially likes to write about animals. Susan lives in Cabot, Arkansas, with her husband, Michael, and many pets.

ABOUT THE ILLUSTRATOR

Robert Squier has been drawing dinosaurs ever since he could hold a crayon. Today, instead of using crayons, he uses pencils, paint, and the computer. Robert lives in New Hampshire with his wife, Jessica, and a house full of dinosaur toys. *Stegosaurus* is his favorite dinosaur.